The Okanagan

The Okanagan

Photographs by Hugo Redivo

Introduction by Eric Sismey

Toronto
OXFORD UNIVERSITY PRESS
1978

To my wife Dorothy and our children
Marcus, Selwyn, Rhea and Franca

My deepest thanks go to my family, whose patience and
creative help have made it possible for me to photograph
the Okanagan. Among many others, I owe a special debt
to my late friend Alfred Grundig, who introduced me to
the art of photography. Finally I should like to thank
Roger Boulton and his colleagues, who helped me make
this book and share my vision of the Okanagan.   HR

© Oxford University Press (Canadian Branch) 1978
ISBN 0-19-540286-3
1234-1098
Printed in Hong Kong by
EVERBEST PRINTING COMPANY LIMITED

Introduction

In Southern British Columbia, hidden between the Columbia Mountains and the Cascade Range, is the dry, warm valley of the Okanagan, Skaha, and Osoyoos Lakes. This is a country of vast horizons, fertile grasslands, glittering stretches of brilliant blue water, sandy beaches, mountains and gullies, meadows, cliffs, forests and blossoms. Although it is a land of abundant variety, set under the limitless Western sky, the Okanagan Valley is small in relation to British Columbia as a whole. There are several lakes in the province that could swallow Lake Okanagan. The Canadian part of the valley is only about 130 miles long and it is seldom as much as a dozen miles across. Yet its beauty and diversity give the traveller a sense of scale and grandeur out of all proportion to what he can see on the map.

There are those, even in the valley itself, who are unaware that its southern tip harbours a patch of desert—true Western desert that extends intermittently in the rain shadow of the coastal mountains, south between the high cordilleras, into the Great Basin Desert of Oregon and Nevada. The northern tip of this classical Western region lies in Canada, and is the only such desert north of the border. Here the hills are studded with ponderosa pines. The cactus blossoms, the greasewood puts out its spiny branches, lizards and turtles abound, and the unwary meets with rattlesnakes. The Southern Okanagan gets less than ten inches of rainfall a year. The summer temperatures, though dry, are tropical, and in them flourish birds, flowers, and wildlife that are to be found nowhere else in Canada.

The natural dryness of the valley calls for extensive irrigation, which has transformed it from a range of Bunchgrass into one of the fruit gardens of the continent. Water is drawn from the Okanagan River in the south and in the north from the lakes and surrounding mountain streams. The valley is bordered by mountains— not Alpine, but high enough for heavy snow cover in winter and rugged enough to make demands on hikers who would pick their way among the outcrops of rock. Ski slopes sweep down from the summits, where wild flower gardens blaze with colour well into July, through the upland forests to meet the grasslands below, government descriptions of the region, by the enthusiasm of the Governor General of Canada, Lord Aberdeen, who had bought large tracts of Okanagan land himself, where cattle graze in the summer: beef herds in the southern ranges, dairy herds on the northern slopes. The valley floor is rich with apples, peaches, pears, apricots, cherries, and vines.

The beauty of the Okanagan, the richness of its land, the peace of its shores, have attracted settlers for over a hundred years. The first European to see the valley may have been David Stuart, a pathfinder for the Pacific Fur Company, who boated upstream from the mouth of the Columbia in 1811. Where the Columbia is joined by the Okanogan (in Canada spelled Okanagan), he built Fort Okanogan and then travelled north along the lakes to the Thompson. He had found an excellent land route to unite the Upper Fraser and the Lower Columbia. Now all the vast interior between the Rockies and the Coastal Ranges was open for trade and later for settlement. In 1824 the Okanagan Valley trail was taken by the Hudson's Bay Company Fur Brigade, and until 1847 fur caravans of as many as two hundred pack animals at a time travelled the hills beside the lake each year. Much of the old trail is orchard and vineyard now, much of it town or paved road, but there are still short sections where hikers can follow the route the fur traders took a century and a half ago.

Permanent settlement of the Okanagan began when Father Charles Pandosy of the Oblates of Mary arrived to establish a mission near what is now Kelowna. On the 8th of October 1859 he recorded that 'Last night we arrived at this place which we have chosen for our mission. It is in a great valley near the middle of Great Okanagan Lake. . . The cultivable land is immense.' His mission was the first settlement of the interior to be founded neither on fur nor on gold. His purpose was to convert the native people, to bring them Christianity, to teach them, and to introduce agriculture to this 'immense, cultivable land'. He built his mission and along with it the first school in the interior. He planted potatoes, grapevines, grain, and apple trees. Apples grown from the offshoots of his original plantings are treasured in the Okanagan, though the first orchard in the valley was not planted until 1866 at Penticton by an Irishman, Thomas Ellis.

The big wave of immigration and settlement came in the 1890s. Attracted by and by the advertisements of the CPR for its new services in the valley, settlers began to establish fruit ranches around Kelowna and Vernon. In the next ten years or so a million fruit trees were planted and the acreage increased in value by a thousand-fold. From these beginnings developed an industry that today provides about one third of all the apples grown commercially in Canada. Increasingly now the grape is challenging the apple in prominence, Okanagan grapes being grown both for table fruit and for excellent wines.

Amid all of its modern domesticity and abundant cultivation, the romance of the Old West can still be felt in the Okanagan. Remnants of wooden country stores fade in the sun of the sage-hills. Fragments of early settlement and half-forgotten Indian graveyards lie hidden in the long dry grass. The pioneer stern-wheel steamer *Sicamous* lies beached at Penticton. Country rodeos and Indian festivals recall the past.

The Okanagan today is a lively playground all year round. There is good fishing in the open lakes among the mountain forests; sailing, boating, and waterskiing on the lakes below. In the summer the population of the valley doubles with the coming of the tourists, many of them attracted by the warm swimming and by sunbathing on the long sandy beaches. Several highlights of the summer season are known far beyond the borders of British Columbia. The Peach Festival at Penticton is a week of parades, floats, and bands. The Kelowna International Regatta includes over a hundred water events. In August, Penticton hosts the mammoth British Columbia Square Dance Jamboree, which brings enthusiasts from all over North America. In winter the change of season is celebrated by the Winter Carnival at Vernon.

Hugo Redivo has lived on the shore of Skaha Lake for almost thirty years. His images portray the landscape, flowers, and animals, the pastimes and carnivals, the farming and history of the Okanagan region. This book of his work is meant to portray the Okanagan for all Canadians—for those who live there, for those who visit and wish to return (as many do when the time comes for them to retire), and for those who have yet to discover this golden land.   ERIC SISMEY

1   Without irrigation, there would be no grass for haymaking.
This hayfield overlooks Kalamalka Lake, south of Vernon.

2 Calm water and a sailboat against the morning haze.

3 Highway 97 winds along Okanagan Lake. There are stretches of the
highway where the cliffs barely leave
room for it. In other places ancient
mud slides have left spits that make
pleasant picnic grounds.

4 (*left*) Mount Nkwala, named in memory of an Indian Chief.

5 Skaha Lake, looking towards Kaleden.

6 (*left*) A roadside encounter in the early-morning sun.

7 By the time the peach trees are in bloom, dandelions are thick in the orchard grass.

8   Bunchgrass sprouting from a crack in parched soil.

9   (*right*) Open flowers and buds of the Bitter Root, which grows in the driest of places.

10 Confluence of the Okanagan River with Skaha Lake.

11   Evening by the lake.

12 A white fence, a saddle and a
horse reflect a treasured Okanagan
lifestyle.

13   This little tower on top of an old barn at Trout Creek, Summerland, once housed a pulley that hoisted hay up to the loft.

14   Balsam Roots—or 'Okanagan Sunflowers', as they are called locally—cover the hills with bright yellow flowers throughout the spring and into the summer. The native Indians used the roots, shoots, and seeds for food.

15   (*right*) Seemingly endless roads that beckon beyond the horizon are as much a symbol of the Okanagan as they are of all the Canadian West.

16 (*left*) Dry hillsides are spiked with low-growing 'Prickly Pear' cactus, seen here in full bloom.

17 Much of the shoreline of Okanagan Lake consists of 'claycliffs' built of fine silt left by the glaciers of the Ice Age. Here they tower above a slope of Greasewood.

18 While the apple trees are in full bloom, there is still skiing on the mountains. Mount Apex is seen here on the horizon.

19 (*right*) A canter across a plateau and a steep climb to the next. The rugged mountains enclosing the Okanagan Valley are fun to explore on horseback.

20   (*left*) Originally just a resting
place for migrant waterbirds, the
Okanagan is more and more becom-
ing a permanent home and breeding
place for Canada Geese.

21   Though the Okanagan is in the
'dry belt' of British Columbia, there
are many swampy pockets of unex-
pected greenery in side valleys, low-
lands, and along the banks of creeks.
The ecology of the Valley is very
delicate.

22   A forgotten store in a deserted village.

23   (*right*) Skaha Lake looking towards Penticton. This view is typical of the Okanagan in the spring—a clear sky, blue lakes, pale green hillsides, and rolling wooded mountains.

24 Small, unpretentious Yellow Bells
bloom in early spring, rewarding the
hiker with their gentle beauty.

25　These orange-painted boxes await delivery of the daily *Penticton Herald*.

26 Dairy farms are in the northern Okanagan, where the meadows need little or no irrigation. This is a typical scene north of Vernon.

27 This old clapboard house
at Vernon still shows some pride.

28 Finding these abandoned wagon wheels—a reminder of
'good old times'—someone may very well use them as garden props,
or even as a conversation piece inside the house.

29   The propeller of an old 'putt-putt' boat.

30 Strong, dusty windstorms occasionally sweep up or down the Valley. This one hit Penticton's Main Street, creating a strange effect of wind and light.

31 This old gas pump, looking like an artifact on display in an outdoor museum, is still in use—another reminder of changing times.

32   Young Indians in traditional
Salish costume take part in local
festivities.

33 Cat Tails, wild raspberries, small Golden Rod and Pale Everlasting thrive in confusion and share the available moisture along a creek.

34 White apricot blossoms burst from their reddish buds.

35 Some windblown seeds of Holly-
hock from a nearby garden came to
grow along the roadside and mix with
the weeds.

36 The fruit industry has its ups and
downs. Some orchards have had to
give way to different uses; others wait
to be sold. In the meantime, farm
animals enjoy the lush grass.

37   The Okanagan River used to meander along the Valley
until a canal was built to straighten it and control its flow
to prevent flooding.

38 Oregon Grapes are a delight all year around. In the spring they bear golden clusters of flowers. In the summer such berries as the birds don't eat make delicious jam. In the winter the shiny green leaves make decorations for the home.

39 Peaches demand great care. Each peach must be picked by experienced hands at just the right moment, when it is ripe enough for taste but still firm enough to stand up to packing and shipping.

40 (*left*) Highway 97 crosses Okanagan Lake, between Westbank and
Kelowna, over this floating bridge.
Rapidly expanding Kelowna stretches
from the shores of the lake into the
hills.

41 A friendly welcome outside the
Civic Centre in Vernon.

42 Gnarled pine branches frame the view across a dry meadow of Bunch-grass to the waters of Skaha Lake.

43 (*right*) The S.S. *Sicamous* plied the waters of Okanagan Lake in regular service until 1935. Highways replaced her for transportation and she is moored now in Penticton, where she serves as a restaurant.

44 Parades—every community has it's annual celebration: the Armstrong Fall Fair, the Vernon Winter Carnival, the Kelowna Regatta, the Oliver Horse Show, Penticton's Peach Festival (shown here), and many others.

45   At Penticton in July the Okanagan Summer School of the Arts offers
instruction, and some of the students
are seen here on a field trip to the Indian village.

46 Bunchgrass, the perennial that dots these hill-sides, is living hay and very good nourishment for livestock. The 'bunches' grow new blades of green grass in the spring, but in the first heat of June they turn yellow.

47 Exciting rodeos such as this one are as popular in the
Okanagan as anywhere else in the West.

48 Ripe apples in autumn cast a rich, fermenting smell of fruit upon the air on sunny days. Apples are the main crop of the Valley's fruit industry.

49   A Square Dance Jamboree is held every year in
Penticton, drawing over three thousand dancers and
lasting a full week. There are parades and dancing in
the streets or by the lake. In the evening everybody
gathers on the large wooden dance floor in the open
air to swirl and 'do-si-do' to the best callers.

50 (*left*) Dawn, between Peachland and Kelowna.

51 The dry summer season brings danger, for the woods will explode at the drop of a smouldering match. Lightning storms also leave their mark, and the accompanying rains are seldom enough to put out the fires.

52 (*left*) In these rocky hills, access to fires is often difficult. Waterbombers help firefighters from the air, or if possible put out a fire with chemicals before it spreads.

53 Because of its colour and drama, a forest fire can have a strange and beautiful fascination for the photographer, disastrous though it is.

54   A glimpse away from the lakes into a side valley and up to the rolling mountains beyond. This is Prairie Valley, Summerland.

55   (*right*) Miles of sandy beaches welcome local people and tourists alike. The population of the Valley doubles in the summer months. Even so, this beach on Skaha Lake does not appear crowded.

56 Vineyards are the newest addition
to the variety of commercial fruit-growing. This one is east of Oliver, but
they are cultivated as far north as
Kelowna. The Research Station of the
Canada Department of Agriculture
in Summerland is very much involved,
among other things, with testing and
developing new varieties of grapes.

40 (*left*) Highway 97 crosses Okanagan Lake, between Westbank and
Kelowna, over this floating bridge.
Rapidly expanding Kelowna stretches
from the shores of the lake into the
hills.

41 A friendly welcome outside the
Civic Centre in Vernon.

42   Gnarled pine branches frame the view across a dry meadow of Bunch-grass to the waters of Skaha Lake.

43   (*right*) The S.S. *Sicamous* plied the waters of Okanagan Lake in regular service until 1935. Highways replaced her for transportation and she is moored now in Penticton, where she serves as a restaurant.

44 Parades—every community has it's annual celebration: the Armstrong Fall Fair, the Vernon Winter Carnival, the Kelowna Regatta, the Oliver Horse Show, Penticton's Peach Festival (shown here), and many others.

45 At Penticton in July the Okanagan Summer School of the Arts offers instruction, and some of the students are seen here on a field trip to the Indian village.

46 Bunchgrass, the perennial that dots these hillsides, is living hay and very good nourishment for livestock. The 'bunches' grow new blades of green grass in the spring, but in the first heat of June they turn yellow.

47   Exciting rodeos such as this one are as popular in the
Okanagan as anywhere else in the West.

48   Ripe apples in autumn cast a rich, fermenting smell of fruit upon the air on sunny days. Apples are the main crop of the Valley's fruit industry.

49   A Square Dance Jamboree is held every year in Penticton, drawing over three thousand dancers and lasting a full week. There are parades and dancing in the streets or by the lake. In the evening everybody gathers on the large wooden dance floor in the open air to swirl and 'do-si-do' to the best callers.

50 (*left*) Dawn, between Peachland and Kelowna.

51 The dry summer season brings danger, for the woods will explode at the drop of a smouldering match. Lightning storms also leave their mark, and the accompanying rains are seldom enough to put out the fires.

52 (*left*) In these rocky hills, access to fires is often difficult. Waterbombers help firefighters from the air, or if possible put out a fire with chemicals before it spreads.

53 Because of its colour and drama, a forest fire can have a strange and beautiful fascination for the photographer, disastrous though it is.

54 A glimpse away from the lakes into a side valley and up to the rolling mountains beyond. This is Prairie Valley, Summerland.

55 (*right*) Miles of sandy beaches welcome local people and tourists alike. The population of the Valley doubles in the summer months. Even so, this beach on Skaha Lake does not appear crowded.

56 Vineyards are the newest addition to the variety of commercial fruit-growing. This one is east of Oliver, but they are cultivated as far north as Kelowna. The Research Station of the Canada Department of Agriculture in Summerland is very much involved, among other things, with testing and developing new varieties of grapes.

57   Some of the grape harvesting is still done by hand, but more and more growers of large vineyards are changing over to harvesting machines.

58   A cluster of De Chaunac grapes
ready to be harvested and turned
into red wine. The average yield is
between five and six tons from
one acre.

59   Several wineries process the grapes of the Valley into a wide variety of wines. These outdoor stainless-steel holding tanks, thirty of them, can store 25,000 gallons each. They belong to Casabello Wines Ltd. in Penticton.

60 (*left*) Wherever there is a patch of wet ground,
Bullrushes stick their dark, slender heads skyward
and release their cottony seeds to the wind.

61   Turtles are native to some of the small mountain lakes,
such as Sleepy Waters in the Southern Okanagan.

62 Stray seeds of the Common Mullein found a place to grow in this abandoned orchard. The pale yellow of this wild grass is a typical colour of the Okanagan countryside in late summer and fall.

63   Indian cemetery beside the Mission Church near Penticton. It is not much more than a hundred years since white people came to this Valley and brought an enormous change to the small, peaceful settlements along the Okanagan River.

64 The life of the Okanagan is enriched by several active Indian communities. Here Salish Coast Indians, come to visit on a festive weekend, prepare salmon they have brought.

65 (*right*) The salmon fillets, skewered on sticks and barbecued over open fires, were complemented by other dishes and served to the public by members of the local Indian band.

66   A giraffe at the Okanagan Game Farm in Kaleden. The farm is populated with North American and other exotic wild animals from all over the world. Besides being a tourist attraction, it is used for film-making and has become important for scientific research to the University of British Columbia and Simon Fraser University, as well as to the Fish and Wildlife Branch of the Government of British Columbia.

67   The Dominion Radio Astrophysical Observatory of the National Research Council of Canada at White Lake, built in 1959. The 25-metre-wide 'dish' is used to study the radio signals from a variety of astronomical objects—from sources distributed throughout our own galaxy as well as from the very distant radio galaxies and quasars.

68 Quiet lakes in the dense mountain
forests offer good and varied fishing.
Many of them are easily accessible
and have camping facilities, such as
those at Headwaters, behind Peachland.

69 Oyama is where Kalamalka Lake and Woodlake meet. 'Kalamalka' is the Indian way of saying 'lake of many colours'.

70 (*left*) This old farm, surrounded by the green meadows of the Northern Okanagan, tells of a time when farming was more a way of life than a commercial business.

71 The mountains around the Okanagan Valley yield timber for the many sawmills of the area, making lumber another important industry of the Okanagan. This mill is near Lumby.

72 (*left*) This picturesque old boat shelter on Lake Osoyoos may still be usable, but it looks more like a rustic memento of the past.

73 Though garden roses are delicate and pampered, the wild rose grows almost anywhere. The seeds of Rose-hips, beautiful in themselves, are a valuable winter food for all kinds of birds and animals.

74 Sumac—whether the wild variety that grows on the driest hillside or the ornamental Staghorn Sumac of garden and park—flourishes in the Okanagan and lights up the autumn countryside with brilliant red leaves.

75 (*right*) The popular sport of waterskiing could have been invented here. Hours pass unnoticed for spectators and participants alike, until the setting sun or a healthy appetite calls for a rest.

76 (*left*) Autumn day along Okanagan Lake near Summerland.

77 Norway Maple.

78 Moist, rich soil supports the
Scarlet Gilia, which grows up to
three feet tall. Blooming for most of
the summer, the Gilia add vivid
touches of colour to the landscape.

79 Claycliffs along the shore of
Okanagan Lake.

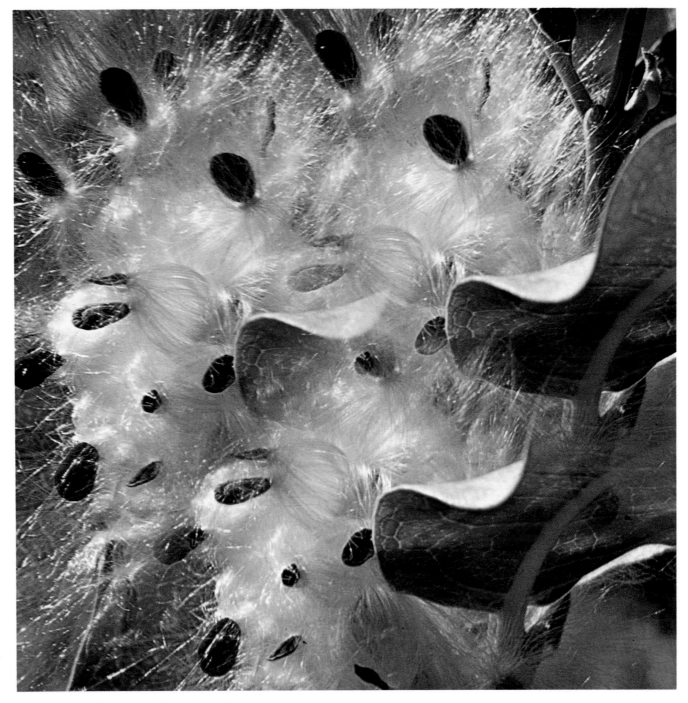

80 (*left*) With the increasing number
of local people engaged in spinning
and weaving, wool is finding a larger
market in the Okanagan. Owing to
the mild climate, however, the
sheep's fleece here does not grow as
long and thick as local spinners
would like.

81 Milkweed make a show along the
roadside, their silky seed pods catch-
ing the light of the setting sun.

82 Fewer and fewer historic buildings, like this 'ghost' house, remain.

83   There was once a lively freight traffic on Okanagan Lake. Tug boats like this one moved barges
loaded with railway cars between communities
on the lake. This particular boat, no longer in use,
is moored at Vernon.

84   (*left*) A good day for skiing need not be sunny.

85   The view from Apex Alpine Park, near Penticton. There is very good skiing in the uplands, with several areas to choose from.

86   On the average, Skaha Lake freezes over once every five years, whereas the larger Okanagan Lake to the north has not been frozen since the winter of 1949-50.

87   (*right*) Beef cattle roam the open range during the summer. In winter they gather at feeding lots such as this one on the Richter Pass in the Southern Okanagan.

88 'Enough!'